T0298806

Food Remittances: Migration and Food Security in Africa

SAMP MIGRATION POLICY SERIES NO. 72

Jonathan Crush and Mary Caesar

Series Editor: Prof. Jonathan Crush

Southern African Migration Programme (SAMP)
2016

AUTHORS

Jonathan Crush is the CIGI Chair in Global Migration and Development at the Balsillie School of International Affairs, Waterloo, Canada.

Mary Caesar is a Post-Doctoral Fellow at the Balsillie School of International Affairs, Waterloo, Canada.

ACKNOWLEDGEMENTS

SAMP wishes to thank the International Fund for Agricultural Development (IFAD) and the International Institute for Environment and Development (IIED) for their funding of this project. This report was also published in the IIED working paper series and is published here with permission from IIED and IFAD. Our thanks to Cecilia Tacoli and Bronwen Dachs for their assistance in preparing this report.

Published by the Southern African Migration Programme, International Migration Research Centre, Balsillie School of International Affairs, Waterloo, Ontario, Canada

First published 2016

ISBN 978-1-920596-19-4

Cover photo by Elles van Gelder/IRIN

Production by Bronwen Dachs Muller, Cape Town

Printed by Megadigital, Cape Town

All rights reserved. No part of this publication may be reproduced or transmitted, in any form or by any means, without prior permission from the publishers

CONTENTS   PAGE

LIST OF TABLES

LIST OF FIGURES

EXECUTIVE SUMMARY

Cash remittances have grown rapidly over the past two decades and are now at an all-time high. The World Bank estimates that international remittances reached USD436 billion in 2014, and predicts that they will increase to USD601 billion in 2016. Studies of remitting practices and impacts often define remittances to include both cash and in-kind (goods) flows. But they invariably ignore the volume, value and impacts of international goods (including food) remitting. When it comes to internal migration, the growing literature on urban-rural linkages might be expected to focus on both cash *and* goods remitting by migrants. However, once again far more attention has been paid to cash than food remitting. There is considerable evidence from across the African continent that a significant proportion of cash remittances to rural areas is spent on food. However, bidirectional food remitting – its drivers, dimensions and impacts – is an underdeveloped research and policy area. This report therefore reviews the current state of knowledge about food remittances in Africa and aims to make a number of contributions to the study of the relationship between migration and food security.

The first section of this report focuses on cross-border food remitting in Africa. Across the continent, there is considerable evidence of a massive informal trade in food, including staples, fresh and processed products. Though informal in nature, most cross-border trade in foodstuffs is a result of commercial transactions by small-scale traders who buy in one country and sell in another. However, not all of the foodstuffs that cross borders informally is destined for markets and purchase by urban and rural consumers. An unknown proportion is actually food remittances on their way from migrants to kin in their country of origin. A SAMP survey of 4,765 migrant-sending households in five SADC countries found that goods remitting was a significant component of overall remittance flows within the region. In total, two-thirds of the households had received cash in the previous year, and just over one-third had also received goods, including foodstuffs. In total, 28% of migrant-sending households across the five countries had received food remittances, with a high of 60% in Mozambique and a low of 8% in Lesotho.

Within countries there is now considerable evidence that urban migrant households rely to varying degrees on an informal, non-marketed supply of food from their rural counterparts to survive in precarious urban environments. Rural-urban links that are fostered and maintained by the migration process are fundamental to the ability of poor urban households to survive. Around one in three of the 6,000 poor urban households in 11 Southern African cities surveyed by the African Food Security Urban Network (AFSUN) in 2008-2009 had received food remittances from relatives or friends outside the city in the year prior to the study. The prevalence of food remitting varied considerably from city to city: Windhoek was highest (at 47% of all households), followed by Lusaka (44%), Harare (42%), Maseru (37%), Blantyre (36%) and Manzini (35%). By contrast, the proportion of urban households receiving food remittances was significantly lower in the three South African cities surveyed.

Though rural-urban food remitting has been shown to be significant in various case studies, urban-urban food remittances have been virtually ignored. In the AFSUN study, while 41% of all households received rural-urban transfers, even more remitting (48%) occurred between urban areas. The reasons why so many urban households receive food remittances either from rural or from urban areas, but not both, requires additional research. Is it a function of how long a migrant has lived in the city, with more recent migrants likely to retain stronger links with the countryside? Or is it related to the fact that migrants receiving food remittances from other urban areas do so primarily from urban centres in other countries? And what is the relationship, if any, between the size of an urban centre and the incidence of food remitting? Certainly the phenomenon of urban-urban food remitting suggests a need to go beyond the standard idea that rural-urban linkages are the only important influence on the food security of urban populations.

There has been only one cross-national comparative study that looks at the rural drivers of foods remittances. The study interviewed 3,388 rural farm households in nine East and Southern African countries and found that 84% were maize producers and 35% were maize remitters. The most common type of food remitting was rural-rural (to neighbouring villages and other rural areas). In addition, rural-urban food remittances tend to vary with the proximity and size of the destination. Remitting behaviour varied with household income. As household income increased, so did the propensity to remit. At the same time, all households tended to remit a similar proportion of their maize production irrespective of how well off they were. The negative effects of food remitting seem to be much more severe on poorer households.

The two case studies presented in this report are designed to highlight different facets of food remitting with potentially broader applicability. The first case study, of Harare in Zimbabwe, looks at food remittances under conditions of extreme economic and political duress. Zimbabwe's economic meltdown after 2000 is unprecedented but many African countries are no strangers to economic crisis, civil strife and, in some cases, state failure. The significance of food remitting to the urban poor in a state in crisis is amply demonstrated by the Harare case. In addition, the case study allows an assessment of the impact on food remitting of macro-economic and political stabilization. Clearly, without significant improvement in employment levels, incomes and the cost of food, the amelioration of a crisis, in itself, will have only a marginal impact on food remitting.

The Windhoek case study provides an important example of cash and food remittances for food remittances reciprocity. At the same time, it raises a set of hypotheses about food remittances that need further elaboration and testing. These include the relationship between urban poverty and the level of food remitting; whether food remittances substantially reduce levels of urban food insecurity; if the volume and frequency of food remitting is related to the strength of the other links that urban residents maintain with the rural end; the reasons for inter-household variation in levels of food security and food receipts within the same geographical area of the city; the apparent greater vulnerability of female-centred households despite the lack of evidence for gender discrimination in food remitting; and whether reciprocal remitting patterns change over time with increased migration and urbanization.

Based on its survey of existing knowledge, this report draws a number of conclusions about the importance of food remittances and the need for further research on this important topic:

- The literature and policy discussions on the impact of migrant remittances – on global, regional and national scales – focus almost exclusively on cash remitting. Connections between remittances and food tend to be confined to discussions of the impact of cash remittances on rural agricultural production and the widespread use of cash remittances by recipients to purchase food.

- The remitting of goods, and especially foodstuffs, across international boundaries and within countries has received little attention primarily because these flows occur outside market channels. The result is that there is not much solid information on the volume, value and impacts of food remitting.

- The growing literature on urban-rural linkages has highlighted the complexity and dynamism of these connections in the context of rapid urbanization and greatly increased rural-urban migration in Africa. However, informal food remittances as a form of linkage have been neglected in favour of discussions of formal, market-based interactions and other types of flows.

- Urban-rural links involving remittances tend to be bidirectional in nature. Cash remittances tend to be unidirectional (from urban to rural), but food remittances are often bidirectional, with fresh produce flowing one way and processed foods the other. Alternatively, there is an element of reciprocity, with cash remittances flowing one way and food remittances the other.

- There is considerable variability in the volumes, frequency and types of foodstuffs that flow to the towns and cities for reasons that are not yet clear, given that many towns and cities have equally poor and food insecure populations. For example, it is clear why rural-urban food remitting is unimportant in South Africa where nearly 70% of the population is urbanized and the rural smallholder population is extremely impoverished. But why would there be such a large difference between Windhoek and Maputo, for example, when both cities have strong connections to the countryside?

- Rural-urban food remittances tend to focus more on poor urban households and are important to bolstering their food security. While we know a little about the importance of food remitting to urban food security, we know much less about what it means for rural food security in terms both of food sent and received. Finally, while it is important to focus on the rural-urban dimensions of food remitting, we should not ignore the fact that there are also other significant dimensions of food remitting that are relatively unexplored, including rural-rural and urban-urban remitting.

- Policy prescriptions for maximizing the flow and impacts of cash remittances on development are now commonplace. No equivalent knowledge base or policy dialogue exists with regard to food remittances. Much additional research on this important, yet neglected, aspect of urban-rural linkages and informal cross-border transactions is therefore urgently required. By drawing attention to the importance of food remittances for urban and rural food security and identifying the current knowledge gaps, this report creates a platform for the design of a new research and policy agenda.

INTRODUCTION

Globally, the transfer of funds by migrants to their home countries or areas (cash remittances) has grown rapidly over the past two decades. The World Bank estimates that international remittances reached USD436 billion in 2014, and predicts that they will increase to USD601 billion in 2016 (Figure 1).[1] These figures, which exclude transfers through informal channels, far exceed global flows of Official Development Assistance. Comparable data for internal remittance flows is "non-existent" but may significantly exceed international cash remittances.[2] There is much debate about what kinds of impacts these remittances have on the regions where migrants come from and the households that send the cash.[3] Some see remittances as a "new development mantra" and a major driver of macro- and micro-economic development and poverty reduction in countries and areas of migrant origin.[4] Others regard cash remittances as a "curse" with negative effects because they increase dependency, weaken institutional capacity and rarely contribute to overall economic growth.[5]

A recent review of the state of research on the links between migration and development argues that we have now moved "far beyond remittances."[6] But there are still aspects of remitting that have received scant attention – for example, the relationship between migration, remittances and food security.[7] The literature on rural food security in Africa and Asia has recently begun to acknowledge the importance of migration and remitting to mitigating food shortages among rural households.[8] But most of the research in this field focuses on the impact of cash remittances on rural agricultural systems and food production.[9] It is now generally acknowledged that many rural recipients of cash remittances spend a significant proportion of this income on food rather than farming. This undermines the spurious idea that rural areas are agriculturally self-sufficient or have the inherent potential to reach this state with the right dose of "rural development."[10] There is also case study evidence from countries including Ghana and Nigeria that shows that off-farm income (primarily in the form of cash remittances) improves levels of food security among rural households.[11] However, one study argues that at the national level there is no evidence that increased migration leads to better rural food security outcomes in Ghana.[12]

Recent global overviews of remitting practices and impacts do define remittances to include both cash and in-kind (goods) flows.[13] But they then proceed to ignore the latter in the rest of their analyses, a response that is typical in much of the literature on this topic. The economistic bias of the International Monetary Fund (IMF), the World Bank and national governments also fails to consider the volume and impacts of goods remitting, both domestic and international. As a result, researchers and policymakers tend to ignore goods (including food) remitting when discussion turns to the impacts of remittances on development. A World Bank study of the Canada-Caribbean remittance corridor, for example, devoted two brief paragraphs to goods and food remitting in a 163-page report.[14] Even practices such as the sending of barrels containing food and other consumer goods from Canada and the United States to family members in the Caribbean have attracted little serious analysis.[15] One study provides a classic example of the problem, confining its analysis of remittances between Canada and the Caribbean entirely to financial remittances.[16] It is left to one of their informants to note, in passing, that "we have been shipping down barrels, many, many barrels. We sent new stuff, used stuff, perishable items." The invisibility of food remittances is largely because they "run within the family and outside market channels."[17]

Figure 1: Global Cash Remittance Flows, 1990–2014

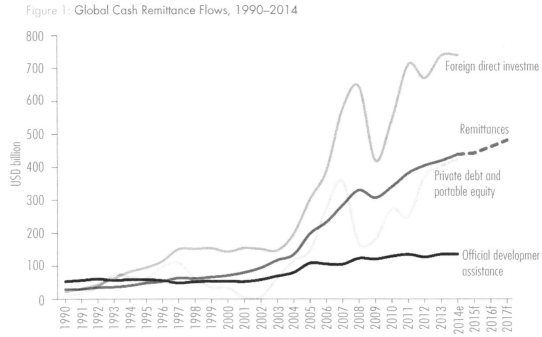

Source: World Bank (2015: 4)

The growing inter-disciplinary literature on urban-rural linkages might be expected to focus on the remitting of both cash and goods by migrants. After all, urban-rural linkages involve the "reciprocal flows of people, goods, services, money and environmental services between rural and urban locations."[18] Certainly, the importance of cash remittances to rural food purchase is acknowledged. A growing number of rural people buy more food than they sell and "these net food buyers are typically from low-income groups who rely on access to affordable food and the cash to purchase it."[19] But much less attention has been paid to the practice of food remitting. A seminal 1998 study of rural-urban linkages, for example, outlined a variety of bidirectional flows but did not specifically discuss food remitting and its relationship to the food security of urban and rural households.[20] Subsequent studies have tended to follow suit, mostly overlooking the potential importance of food remitting as a key link between rural and urban areas that affects food security in both.[21]

The search for a "wider lens" on the nature of urban and rural linkages therefore needs to move beyond cash-based, market transactions and consider bidirectional flows of goods, including foodstuffs, and their impact on the food security of urban and rural populations. These linkages, and the way they are being reconfigured by the rapid urbanization of the South, require much more attention from researchers and policymakers interested in the transformation of rural-urban linkages and the implications for food security of rural and urban residents. Research on rural-urban linkages has increasingly abandoned the dualistic idea that the urban and the rural are discrete and bounded spatial entities: "the notion of a 'rural-urban divide' is increasingly misleading, and oversimplifies a reality, which is more akin to a complex web of relations and connections incorporating rural and urban dimensions and all that is in between – often termed the peri-urban interface."[22] Bidirectional food remittances are an essential but under-explored component of this "complex web" that characterizes economic and social life across the global South.

Despite the general context of Africa's rapid urban transition, it is important not to view rural-urban migration as a one-time relocation of all members of a household. Circular migration – of varying periodicity and spatiality – is still very much the norm in many parts of the continent.[23] The key conceptual question is what kinds of social unit do migrants circulate between? Rather than viewing this in binary terms – as movement between separate and discrete rural and urban households – it can be more productive to see the household as dispersed or "stretched" over space, across the rural-urban divide and very often between countries. Concepts of the divided or stretched household and multi-local household livelihoods are an important starting point for any analysis of the dynamics of food remitting.[24]

A household's multi-local strategies involve "spreading assets and activities in both rural and urban areas, sometimes in the form of circular migration, at other times re-organizing their households as multi-local units with members living and working in different locations but sharing common assets [and that] crossing rural-urban boundaries is an important strategy to reduce vulnerability for both rural and urban poor."[25] Bidirectional and multidirectional food remitting can also be seen as a form of intra-household transfer rather than a set of transfers between different households.[26] But it is important to stress that not all remittances, and not all food remitting, occur within multi-local or "stretched" households. While remittances tend to flow to immediate family, there is also evidence of remitting to households of relatives. A migrant, and especially those who have lived in urban areas for a long time, may well have their own discrete, nuclear or extended household in the urban area and remit to other households (such as that of an elderly parent).

Because food remitting is an underdeveloped research area, there is limited evidence on which to construct a clear picture of its drivers, dimensions and impacts. This report therefore reviews the current state of knowledge about food remittances in Africa. It aims to contribute to the study of changing urban-rural linkages by expanding the geographic and thematic scope of research, demonstrating the value of examining the links between informal food transfers and urban-based household food security, and arguing for a new research and policy agenda focused on food remitting. The first section of the report focuses on international migration within the African continent and associated flows of cash and food remittances.

INTERNATIONAL MIGRATION AND FOOD REMITTANCES

Much of the literature on rural-urban linkages assumes that they are bounded by the borders of the country concerned. Yet many countries in Africa send migrants to, and receive remittances from, other countries in the North and the South.[27] Of Africa's 25 million international migrants, as many as 13 million (53%) are estimated to live in other countries on the continent. Eleven of the top 15 destinations for African migrants are within Africa (Table 1). In 2005, Africa received an estimated USD19 billion in cash remittances, of which USD2.1 billion were from other African countries.[28] The volume of goods and food remitting is undocumented and unknown.

Most migrants who remit across borders within Africa earn income in the urban areas of the countries to which they have moved and then remit to relatives in both rural and urban areas "back home". The potential significance of international cash remitting for food security is suggested by cross-national comparative surveys conducted by the Southern African Migration Programme (SAMP) and the World Bank. SAMP's Migration and Remittances Survey (MARS) in five Southern African countries (Botswana, Lesotho, Mozambique, Swaziland and Zimbabwe) in 2005-2006 found, for example, that 82% of migrant-sending households had purchased food with cash remittances in the previous year and that 81% of household purchases of food by value were paid with remittances.[29] The World Bank's Africa Migration Project surveyed households in Burkina Faso, Kenya, Nigeria, Senegal and Uganda in 2010 and found that a significant proportion of remittances was spent on human and physical capital investments, including food.[30] In each country, a greater proportion of internal rather than international cash remittances was spent on food. In Kenya, for example, the proportion of cash remittances spent on food was 30% for internal remittances, 14% for South-South remittances and 13% for North-South remittances. The equivalent figures in Senegal were 82%, 72% and 63%.

Table 1: Top Destinations of International African Migrants

Country	African-Born Migrants
France	3,048,721
*Cote d'Ivoire	2,261,097
Saudi Arabia	1,341,232
Germany	1,086,997
*Burkino Faso	1,033,450
United States	931,241
United Kingdom	842,246
*Tanzania	828,234
*Sudan	774,350
*South Africa	729,498
*Guinea	669,052
*Nigeria	643,234
*Ethiopia	635,176
*Uganda	511,907
*Ghana	502,496
*= African destination country	
Source: Chikanda and Crush (2014: 71)	

9

To focus exclusively on the use of cash remittances for food purchase is to miss another crucial dimension of the relationship between migration and food security: food remittances across international boundaries. This is clearly a problematic assumption in Africa where there is so much cross-border movement of foodstuffs. Across the continent, there is considerable evidence of a massive informal trade in food, including staples, fresh and processed products.[31] Informal sector cross-border trade (ICBT) is dominated by women, though there are signs of greater male participation in food trading and associated gender struggles over control of the food trade.[32] Though informal in nature, ICBT is animated by commercial transactions by small-scale entrepreneurs at point of purchase in one country and sale in another. One of the complications of monitoring ICBT at borders is that not all of the foodstuffs that cross informally are destined for markets and purchase by urban and rural consumers in the countries of destination. An unknown proportion of the informal trade in foodstuffs is actually food remittances on their way from migrants to kin in their country of origin.

Evidence on the magnitude of cross-border cash and food remitting in Southern Africa comes from a survey of 4,765 cross-border migrant-sending households in five countries. The survey found that goods remitting was a significant component of overall remittance flows within the Southern African Development Community (SADC) region.[33] In total, two-thirds of the households had received cash in the previous year, and inter-country variation in cash remitting was relatively minor (Table 2). The proportion of cash remittances spent on food was 37%, with considerable inter-country variation from a high of 67% in Mozambique to a low of 28% in Lesotho. Just over one-third of the households had also received goods in the previous year. Here again there was considerable variation from country to country. Goods remittances were most important to households in Zimbabwe (68%) and Mozambique (65%) and least important to households in Lesotho (20%) and Swaziland (17%). The average annual value of cash remittances was about three times higher than goods remittances, though in Mozambique they were virtually identical and in Zimbabwe only twice as high. These figures suggest that cash remitting is important to more households but that goods remitting is still significant.

For the purposes of this report, it is more important to know the proportion of households that received food remittances as part of the goods package. The survey showed that a wide variety of goods were remitted, of which clothing and food were by far the most important. In total, 28% of migrant-sending households across the five countries had received food remittances, with a high of 60% in Mozambique and a low of 8% in Lesotho. The low figure for Lesotho may seem surprising given the impoverished state of agriculture in that country, but Lesotho also had the highest proportion of cash remittances spent on food of all the countries surveyed.[34] This suggests that the country's proximity to and integration into the South African economy means that food is readily available, provided that a household has the cash to purchase it.

Table 2: Cash, Goods and Food Remittances in Southern Africa

	Botswana	Lesotho	Mozambique	Swaziland	Zimbabwe	Total
Cash remittances						
Cash remittances (% of households)	76.3	95.3	76.8	64.4	83.5	66.3
Average annual cash remittances (ZAR)	10,413	9,094	2,607	6,279	2,760	6,407
% of cash remittances spent on food	31.5	28.3	66.7	59.5	34.2	37.0
% of food expenditures paid with cash remittances	82.9	90.3	78.1	72.3	79.7	80.8
Goods remittances						
Goods remittances (% of households)	53.2	20.0	64.8	16.6	68.1	33.6
Average annual value of goods remittances	4,853	2,488	2,272	1,838	1,307	2,274
Food remittances						
Food remittances (% of households)	19.8	7.6	60.4	22.0	44.5	28.5
Source: SAMP						

Other research, such as SAMP's Migration and Poverty Survey, has compared domestic and cross-border remitting patterns in the Southern African region by examining internal as well as international migration.[35] This survey canvassed 9,032 households through national surveys in Botswana, Lesotho, Malawi, Mozambique, Namibia, Swaziland and Zimbabwe. Of these, 49% were migrant-sending households. A total of 1,900 households had international migrants (42% of migrant-sending households), 2,134 (or 48%) had internal migrants and 436 (10%) had both. The vast majority of households (between 90%

and 95% in both cases) regarded remittances as important or very important for household survival. Though information was collected on goods remitting, the types of goods were not disaggregated. The regional data set showed that households with international migrants were more likely to receive both cash and goods remittances than internal migrants: 68% of international and 44% of internal migrant-sending households received cash remittances, and 36% of international and 19% of internal migrant-sending households received goods remittances (Table 3). Based on the earlier MARS survey, it is likely that a significant proportion of the goods comprised foodstuffs.

Table 3: International and Internal Remittances in Southern Africa, 2008

	International	Internal
No. of migrant households	1,900	2,134
% receiving cash remittances	68	44
% receiving goods remittances	36	19
Mean cash remittances (ZAR)	4,821	5,434
Mean value of goods remittances (ZAR)	1,702	2,004
Importance to survival (%)	88	85
Source: SAMP		

Other studies of international migrants in South Africa corroborate the importance of food remitting as a livelihood strategy. One study of 487 households compared the remitting behaviour of internal and international migrants in Johannesburg.[36] Three-quarters of the internal migrants were living in an informal settlement (compared with only 11% of the international migrants). Most of the international migrants (86%) lived in the inner city, often in multi-household flats. Just over half of all the households in the total sample remitted money and another 21% sent food. However, international migrants were more likely to remit both cash (60%) and food (30%) than internal migrants (38% cash and 6% food).

INTERNAL MIGRATION AND FOOD REMITTANCES

There is now considerable evidence that urban migrant households rely to varying degrees on an informal, non-marketed supply of food from their rural counterparts to survive in precarious urban environments. Rural-urban links that are fostered and maintained by the migration process "are fundamental to the ability of poor urban households to survive."[37] In Kenya, for example, there is evidence of extensive remitting of cash, clothing, building materials, agricultural equipment and items for funerals from town to countryside and reciprocal remitting of foodstuffs – such as green maize, local vegetables, sweet potatoes, cassava, maize and millet flour, groundnuts, fruits and chicken – from countryside to town.[38]

Around one in three of the 6,000 poor urban households in 11 Southern African cities surveyed by the African Food Security Urban Network (AFSUN) in 2008-2009 had received food remittances from relatives or friends outside the city in the year prior to the study.[39] The prevalence of food remitting varied considerably from city to city, for reasons that are not altogether clear.[40] Receipts of food remittances were highest in Windhoek (at 47% of all households), followed by Lusaka (44%), Harare (42%), Maseru (37%), Blantyre (36%) and Manzini (35%) (Table 4). By contrast, the proportion of urban households receiving food remittances was significantly lower in the three South African cities surveyed.

Table 4: Food Remittances to Poor Urban Households

	% of all households receiving food remittances	% of recipient households receiving remittances from rural areas	% of recipient households receiving remittances from urban areas only	% of recipient households receiving remittances from both rural and urban areas
Windhoek, Namibia	47	72	12	16
Lusaka, Zambia	44	39	44	17
Harare, Zimbabwe	42	37	43	20
Maseru, Lesotho	37	49	44	7
Blantyre, Malawi	36	38	51	11
Manzini, Swaziland	35	53	40	7
Msunduzi, South Africa	24	15	82	3
Maputo, Mozambique	23	23	62	15
Gaborone, Botswana	22	70	16	14
Johannesburg, South Africa	14	24	67	9
Cape Town, South Africa	18	14	83	3
Source: AFSUN				

The survey showed that food transfers were particularly important for food-insecure urban households. Of the 1,809 households receiving food transfers from outside the city, 84% were food insecure and 16% were food secure.[41] Around 80% of households receiving food transfers said that they were important or very important to the household, while 9% said they were critical to household survival. Seventy-seven percent said that the food was sent to help the urban household's food needs, while 20% said the food was sent as a gift. The importance of food transfers to urban food consumption was illustrated by the fact that only 3% of households receiving food sold it, while the rest consumed the food themselves.

COMPARING RURAL-URBAN AND URBAN-URBAN FOOD REMITTANCES

The importance of food remittances for urban food-insecure households was not especially contingent on whether the food was received from rural areas or other urban areas; both were important for recipient households. Though rural-urban food remitting was significant (at 41% of all households receiving transfers), even more remitting (48%) occurred between urban areas. Only a small number (around 11%) received food remittances from both areas. In Gaborone, for example, households were more likely to be food-secure if they received food from rural sources (33%), compared with either urban only (7%) or combined urban and rural sources (8%). But in Maputo just one percent of food-secure households received food from rural areas only compared with 17% of food-secure households getting food from urban areas only (mostly from migrants in South African cities) and the rest from both sources.

In three of the cities, more than half of the recipient households received food remittances from rural areas only: Windhoek (72%), Gaborone (70%) and Manzini (53%). Around half of the Maseru recipients received food from rural areas. Since these four cities are among the smaller centres surveyed by AFSUN, this suggests that rural-urban food remitting might be stronger in countries with lower rates of urbanization, in so-called "secondary cities" with populations of less than 500,000 and possibly in countries with more viable rural smallholder agricultural production. In stark contrast, the proportion of recipient households receiving food remittances from the countryside in all three South African cities was very much lower: at 24% in Johannesburg, 15% in Msunduzi and 14% in Cape Town. The relative unimportance of rural-urban food remitting in South Africa may be because the country is the most urbanized of the nine countries in the study, that these three are larger urban conurbations, and that the rural areas are so impoverished that they do not produce excess food that can be sent to support migrants in the city.

There was also considerable inter-city variation in the relative importance of urban-urban food remitting (Table 4). While recipients of rural-urban food remittances in Windhoek made up 72% of total transfers, urban-urban remittance recipients made up only 12%. In Cape Town, on the other hand, the figures were 14% for rural-urban and 83% for urban-urban remittances. More than 80% of recipients in the other two South African cities also received food from other urban areas. However, it is not only in South Africa that urban-urban food remittances predominate over rural-urban flows. In Maputo, for example, 62% of food remittances received were urban-urban. High rates of urban-urban remitting were also found in Blantyre (51%), Maseru (44%), Lusaka (44%) and Harare (43%). In each case, it was likely that a proportion of transfers came in the form of food remittances from migrants working in one city to their relatives living in another.

The reasons why so many urban households receive food remittances either from rural or from urban areas, but not both, requires additional analysis and explanation. Is it a function of how long a migrant has lived in the city, with more recent migrants likely to retain stronger links with the countryside? Or is it related to the fact that migrants receiving food remittances from other urban areas do so primarily from urban centres in other countries? And what is the relationship, if any, between the size of an urban centre and the incidence of food remitting? Certainly the phenomenon of urban-urban food remitting suggests that we need a more nuanced notion of linkages and flows, which goes beyond the standard idea that rural-urban linkages are the only important influence on the food security of urban populations.

FREQUENCY AND TYPES OF FOOD REMITTING

In the AFSUN study, the geography of remitting, whether rural-urban or urban-urban, was related to the frequency with which urban households received food remittances. Households receiving food from another urban area did so far more often. Around a quarter of households that received food remittances from other urban areas did so at least once a week (compared with only 5% of households that received food from the rural areas). Some 76% of households received urban-urban remittances at least once every two months, compared with only 40% of households receiving rural-urban remittances (Figure 2). This might suggest that urban-urban networks support mechanisms are stronger than rural-urban ties. Alternatively, transportation is undoubtedly easier between urban areas and urban-urban transfers are also much less likely to be affected by the seasonal agricultural cycle.

Figure 2: Frequency of Food Remittances

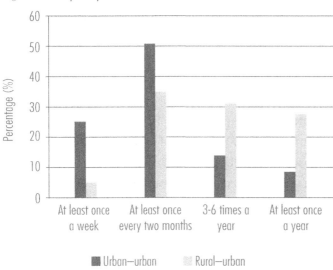

Source: AFSUN

Food remittances from both rural and urban areas are dominated by cereals, primarily maize. All of the recipient urban households in the cities in the AFSUN study received cereals during the year, irrespective of the source. But there was a marked difference in the frequency of transfers, with a quarter of urban-sourced cereals arriving at least once a week and 80% arriving at least once every couple of months or more frequently (Table 5). In contrast, cereals from rural areas came far less frequently, because of the rural agricultural cycle. (Those receiving cereals from other urban areas are not dependent on the cycle since the cereals can be purchased and sent at any time of the year.) In general, the primary difference between rural-urban and urban-urban food remitting is that the former foodstuffs are home produced while the latter are purchased. What impact this has on the food security of producers and purchasers requires additional research.

Table 5: Frequency of Cereals Remitting

Food type	Frequency	Urban–Urban (%)	Rural–Urban (%)
Cereals	At least once a week	27	2
	At least once every 2 months	52	25
	3-6 times a year	12	36
	At least once a year	9	37
Total		100	100
Source: AFSUN			

The types of foodstuffs remitted from rural to urban areas are clearly dependent on the main crops produced by small rural farmers. All of the recipient households received cereals, primarily maize and millet, which are staples in the region. Other agricultural products sent to town included beans/peas/lentils/nuts (40% of recipients), vegetables (37%), roots/tubers (21%) and fruit (9%) (Table 6). Around a quarter of households also received their meat and poultry in the form of food remittances. Urban households receiving food from other urban areas received fewer legumes than those receiving rural-urban transfers. But households receiving urban-urban remittances were more likely to receive all other types of foodstuffs. For example, 51% of households receiving urban-urban transfers received vegetables compared with 37% of those receiving rural-urban transfers. And 39% of urban-urban transfer households received meat or poultry compared with only 23% of rural-urban transfer households. The differences were particularly marked for processed foods such as sugar/honey (40% versus 5%) and foods made with oil, fat or butter (33% versus 6%). There was only minor evidence of rural-urban processed food remitting. This shows that urban-urban remitting is characterized by a greater variety of foodstuffs and is more likely to enhance dietary diversity than rural-urban remitting.

Table 6: Types of Food Remitted

	Rural—Urban % of recipient households	Urban—Urban % of recipient households
Cereals/grain	100	100
Food from beans, peas, lentils, nuts	40	30
Vegetables	37	51
Meat/poultry	23	39
Roots/tubers	21	35
Cheese/milk products	10	18
Fruit	9	19
Foods made with oil, fat, butter	6	33
Sugar/honey	5	40
Eggs	4	14
N	753	890
Source: AFSUN		

FOOD REMITTERS IN RURAL AREAS

There are few large-scale regional studies undertaken about food remitters in rural areas. The best general picture comes from a study by Sweden's Lund University. In 2008, researchers interviewed 3,388 rural farm households in nine African countries: Ethiopia, Ghana, Kenya, Malawi, Mozambique, Nigeria, Tanzania, Uganda and Zambia.[42] They focused on maize remitting and found that 2,857 households (or 84%) were maize producers and that 1,192 (35%) remitted maize to relatives. The proportion of maize-remitting households varied from a high of 69% in Nigeria to a low of 22% in Tanzania.

The Lund study makes three main contributions to the emerging literature on food remittances. First, it shows that the geography of remitting is more complex than suggested by the traditional rural-urban and urban-urban binary (Table 7). They show, for example, that the most frequent type of remitting is rural-rural (to neighbouring villages and other rural areas). In addition, rural-urban food remittances tend to vary with the proximity and size of the destination. About the same proportion of households (just over one-third in each case) send remittances to towns within and outside the district. But much fewer remit to the capital city (23%) and other major urban centres (17%). These figures also suggest that households not only remit to other rural areas but that some remit to more than one destination.

Table 7: Maize Remittance Destinations

	% of remitting households
Neighbouring villages	47
Other rural areas	31
Towns in same district	35
Towns outside district	34
Capital city	23
Major urban centres	17
Source: Andersson Djurfeldt (2015a: 538)	

Second, the Lund study found that food remitting varies with rural household income. As household income increases, so does the propensity to remit. The proportion of households with access to non-farm income (largely cash remittances) varied from 30% for those in the lowest income quintile to 76% for those in the highest income quintile (Table 8). The proportion of households that remit maize increased from 27% in the lowest quintile to 55% in the highest quintile. The total amount of maize remitted also increased with household income, from 117kg for those in the lowest quintile to 321kg for those in the upper quintile. As the research concluded: "The notion that transfers are concentrated among the poorest is to some extent refuted."[43]

Table 8: Maize Remittances and Rural Household Income

	% with access to non-farm income	Mean maize production (kg)	% of households remitting	% of total production remitted	Mean amount of maize remitted (kg)
Quintile 1	30	649	27	18	117
Quintile 2	35	805	36	15	121
Quintile 3	45	1,277	42	15	192
Quintile 4	53	1,768	49	11	195
Quintile 5	76	3,211	55	10	321
Total	51	1,746	42	13	227

Source: Andersson Djurfeldt (2015b)

Third, there is a clear relationship between access to household income and the amount of maize produced. This refutes the common argument that increased off-farm income tends to depress food production. It also shows that despite large differences in average household production across the income quintiles, there is no statistically significant relationship between household income and amount remitted. In other words, all households tend to remit a similar proportion of their maize production irrespective of how well off they are. This suggests that there is a "distributional dualism of food transfers: households in the lower income quintiles are clearly forfeiting their own food security to be able to feed family members and relatives outside the co-resident household and in this sense are not transferring according to their capacity."[44]

The implications of food remitting for the food security of both senders and recipients are not well researched. But the Lund case studies of particular local areas do suggest hypotheses for further exploration. One is that better-off rural households distribute surplus production, while the poorest households support vulnerable family members by sacrificing part of their own subsistence needs via small food gifts.[45] The effects of food remitting seem to be much more severe on poorer households. A paper on remitting from six rural villages in the Nyeri and Kakamega districts of Kenya found that between a third and a half of the sampled households remitted maize: "Transfers may represent a mechanism for counteracting food shortages, price shocks and volatility for receiving households under a system in which markets cannot be trusted to deliver, or do so at seasonally inflated prices" and that they "appeared to act as a parallel informal system of social security in the absence of formal systems guaranteeing a certain measure of food security for vulnerable households."[46]

Another study of eight villages in Malawi found that between 30% and 64% of maize producers were also maize remitters.[47] The study found that maize sellers were more likely to remit than non-sellers, and both selling and remitting were positively correlated with total household production. Among poorer households "remittances take out a relatively large proportion of total production for already food-insecure households, pushing them below their non-remitting counterparts." Echoing the Kenya findings, there were two very different scenarios at work among maize remitters:

> *The sending of remittances appears to point in two different directions on the part of the senders: on the one hand the most affluent and food secure households engage in remittances as a widening of family consumption over space, without compromising the resident household's ability to feed itself. On the other hand, the more vulnerable households undermine the food security of the co-resident household unit to support family members outside the village.*[48]

Another issue is rural-rural food remitting to migrants who have migrated to other rural areas to work or farm. In the Upper West Region of Ghana, for example, food remitting has a "major influence" on the amount of food consumed and on the frequency and type of food eaten.[49] The importance of this study is also the suggestion that food remitting is not simply about material needs and food security but that it has a significant cultural dimension, with food remittances symbolizing the continuity and strength of kin relationships with relatives who live elsewhere. Wives "left behind" by spouses "gauged their husbands' affection from the regularity and amount of food flows they received."[50] The study noted that food from migrant husbands is shared with in-laws to build stronger bonds and strengthen marital ties.

CASE STUDY ONE
FOOD REMITTING IN A STATE OF CRISIS: ZIMBABWE

The inter-connections between urbanization, migration and rural-urban linkages in the first 20 years of Zimbabwean independence have been well documented.[51] The post-2000 economic and political crisis in Zimbabwe, which plumbed new depths in 2008, is also well documented.[52] The crisis led to the mass exodus of people to neighbouring countries such as Botswana and South Africa, as well as to Australia, Canada, the United Kingdom and the United States.[53] By 2008, with formal unemployment in the country running at more than 80% and rampant inflation destroying any residual value held by the Zimbabwean dollar, cash remittances from other countries had become essential to household survival and to the Zimbabwean economy as a whole. Internally, the crisis led to a slowing of urbanization, increased circular migration and intensification of rural-urban linkages.[54]

Flows of cash (especially from South Africa) were complemented by flows of foodstuffs, particularly as many formal retail outlets in Zimbabwe had empty shelves. But what impact did the crisis have on patterns of internal cash and food remitting between urban and rural areas? And did a general change in macro-economic circumstances and the resolution, albeit partial, of the crisis impact on household food security, urban-rural linkages and remitting practices? Research in Epworth, Harare, in 2008, combined with the data from the AFSUN household food security surveys in 2008 and 2012 in three other low-income areas of the city, helps answer both questions.[55]

In 2008, Harare's poor were among the most food insecure in the whole SADC region. The Household Food Insecurity Access Scale (HFIAS) score, which shows the prevalence of food insecurity, was an extremely high 14.7 for the 462 households interviewed by AFSUN in the Harare suburbs of Mabvuku, Tafara and Dzivarasekwa.[56] On the HFIAS scale, only 2% of households were food secure and 72% were severely food insecure (Table 9). The situation in nearby Epworth was a little better, at 3% and 59% respectively.[57] Dietary diversity was also low with two-thirds of the households in the AFSUN survey scoring 5 or less on a scale from 0 to 12 and 29% scoring 3 or less. Similarly, in Epworth, the mean Household Dietary Diversity Scale (HDDS) score was 4.2. Narrow household diets "reflected a deeper food security problem … than prevalence measures alone are able to indicate."[58] All of the households consumed sadza (mealie meal porridge) and a vegetable relish (94%); the other two main components of the diet were foods made with oil and fat (66%) and sugar (58%).

Table 9: Prevalence of Food Insecurity in Harare Low-Income Suburbs, 2008

	Epworth (% of households)	Mabvuku, Tafara, Dzivarasekwa (% of households)
Food secure	3	2
Mildly food insecure	6	3
Moderately food insecure	32	24
Severely food insecure	59	72
N	200	462
Source: Tawodzera (2010); Tawodzera et al (2012)		

The Harare evidence suggests that it is not the mere existence or persistence of urban-rural linkages but their strength that is important to urban livelihoods and food security.[59] In the past, the established practice was for urban households to send money and supplementary food to rural areas. The economic crisis in the country changed the nature of these relationships and remittances from the urban areas, making it harder for them to continue. Many urban households maintained small plots of land in the village to grow crops or keep animals. This became increasingly important as the food crisis worsened in the cities. By engaging in rural farming, urban household members generated food to eat when they visited the countryside or they could sell it to generate a supplementary income for use in both the rural and urban areas. Just over one-third of the households in Epworth visited the rural areas to engage in farming activity.[60]

The strength of the linkages between Harare and the countryside during the crisis was indicated by the frequency of visits and the resource flows between the two. There was a significant relationship between levels of household poverty and the frequency of visits to rural areas, despite increasing costs of travel and declining urban incomes.[61] As many as 64% said that their reason for visiting the rural areas was to get food and/or money. Money from the rural areas was primarily generated by the sale of farm produce or livestock. Urban households were increasingly getting more from the village than they sent, suggesting that the flow of resources between rural and urban areas had reversed. However, it would be incorrect to conclude that this became a one-way flow to Harare. Though the net flow was towards the urban areas, just over a third also said that they visited the rural areas to take money and/or food.

The net flow of resources, and especially food, towards the city was partly responsible for the ability of poor households to remain there, though it is clear that it did not ameliorate overall food insecurity. More than half of the households (61%) surveyed in Epworth in 2008 had received food remittances from the rural areas in the previous year.[62] The most common foods transferred from the rural areas to Epworth included cereals (54% of house-holds), root and tubers (36%), meat and poultry (26%) and food made from beans and nuts (16%) (Figure 3). The high cost of transport between the rural and the urban areas meant that most food transfers were only taking place three to six times a year.

The AFSUN survey found that 29% of low-income households in Harare had received food remittances from the rural areas in the previous year (Figure 4). Cereals were again predominant (at nearly 50% of recipient households), but overall the foodstuffs received were far less diverse than those arriving in Epworth, with lower proportions of all other types of food and very little roots or tubers, fruit, and meat or poultry. AFSUN also found that more households (42%) had received food remittances from other urban areas outside Harare (probably outside the country) than from the rural areas. Of the recipient house-holds, 37% had received food remittances from rural areas only, 43% from urban areas only and 20% from both. This clearly implies that while rural-urban food remitting became important to urban households during a time of severe crisis, food remittances from other urban centres were even more important.

Figure 3: Type and Frequency of Rural–Urban Food Remittances to Epworth, Harare

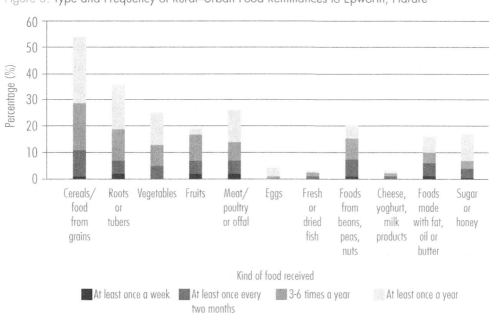

Source: Tawodzera, 2010

23

Figure 4: Types of Food Remittances to Mabvuku, Tafara and Dzivarasekwa, Harare

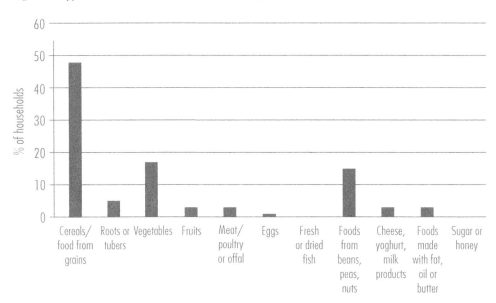

Source: Tawodzera et al (2012)

These studies, conducted at the height of the Zimbabwean crisis, shed light on the nature of reciprocal food and cash remitting during a time of acute economic and social hardship. The Zimbabwean case, therefore, could help in understanding the nature of rural-urban linkages under conditions of state failure and deep crisis in other African contexts. It also raises the question of what happens to these rural-urban linkages and cash and food remittances when a crisis eases or is resolved. To try to answer this question, AFSUN repeated its household survey in the same areas of Harare in 2012 when the worst aspects of the crisis were over. At this time political stability had been restored through a Government of National Unity, the economy was dollarized and inflation had been brought under control. Between 2009 and 2011, Zimbabwe's GDP growth averaged 7.3%, making it one of the world's fastest growing economies, albeit from a very low base. Zimbabwe experienced an economic rebound after 2009 and "with the support of record international price levels, exports of minerals – notably diamonds, platinum, gold, and other products – have injected new life into the economy."[63] Zimbabwean trade flows increased rapidly, with exports (primarily minerals) rising at 39% per year. Imports also rose in response to domestic demand, averaging 34% per year from 2009 to 2011. As the economy stabilized, commercial food production increased and shops restocked with food imported primarily from South Africa.

A comparison of the 2008 and 2012 employment profile of household members suggests little change in the labour market prospects of poor urban households in Harare. Overall employment was only slightly different in 2012 (59% employed) than it had been in 2008 (58% employed).[64] Unemployment figures were also similar (at 42% in 2008 and 40% in 2012). However, among the employed there was a move away from full-time towards part-time employment. The proportion of all working-age adults employed full-time fell from 43% to 35% between 2008 and 2012 and the proportion employed part-time rose from 15% to 24%. Aggregate improvements in household income were reflected in declining levels of food insecurity. For example, the mean household HFIAS fell from 14.7 to 9.6 between 2008 and 2012. This was reflected in the share of food secure and mildly food insecure households increasing from 5% to 17% and the proportion of severely food insecure households falling from 72% to 63% (Table 10). Aggregate household dietary diversity also improved between 2008 and 2012, with the mean HDDS score increasing from 4.8 in 2008 to 6.5 in 2012. But despite the overall improvement in Zimbabwe's macro-economic situation, it is clear that levels of urban household food insecurity remained extremely high in poor neighbourhoods.[65] The question, then, is whether there had been any changes in food remitting practices.

Table 10: Changes in Food Insecurity Prevalence, 2008 and 2012

	2008 (% of households)	2012 (% of households)
Food secure	2	10
Mildly food insecure	3	7
Moderately food insecure	24	20
Severely food insecure	72	63
Total	100	100
Source: AFSUN		

A comparative self-assessment of the importance of food remittances in 2008 and 2012 shows a definite easing over the four-year period (Figure 5). In 2008, for example, more than 70% of the households receiving food remittances said they were either very important or critical to survival. This had fallen to 50% by 2012. Similarly, only 2% of households said that they were unimportant or somewhat important in 2008, compared with 22% in 2012. Overall, then, food remittances remained important for most households but were less critical.

Figure 5: Self-Assessment of Importance of Food Remittances in Harare

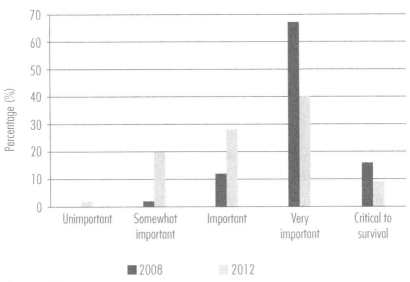

Source: AFSUN

Logically, we might expect that as food remittances become less important, they might also decline in volume and frequency. Interestingly, the proportion of households in the surveyed areas receiving food remittances increased from 42% in 2008 to 47% in 2012 and most of the increase came from rural-urban remitting (from 37% to 42%). But there was a slight drop in the proportion of households receiving food remittances from other urban centres (from 43% to 37%). The proportion receiving food from both rural and urban areas remained virtually the same at around 20%. Although the confiscation of land from white farmers (the Fast Track Land Programme) had a major negative impact on large-scale commercial agriculture in the country, there is an emerging consensus that resettled smallholder farmers are producing a great deal more than they used to. Maize production, for example, increased from 525,000MT in 2008 to 1,450,000MT in 2011. This might explain continued and even increased flows of food remittances. The possibility of harvest-related annual fluctuations means that a definitive answer would require tracking over a much longer time frame. Yet the improved macro-economic situation in 2012 does not appear to have affected the demand for food remittances to a significant degree.

The final question is whether there were any changes in the types of food remitted from rural areas to households in urban Harare. Here there were some interesting shifts (Table

11). In 2008, the top three food types remitted (in terms of the proportion of recipient households receiving that type) were cereals (95%), vegetables (35%) and lentils and nuts (30%). In 2012, cereals were still dominant though there was a drop from 95% to 80% (possibly because maize meal was now more available for purchase in the city), a major drop in vegetables from 35% to 18% (possibly for the same reason), and an increase in roots or tubers (9% to 23%) and fruit (from 5% to 24%) (for reasons that are not clear).

Table 11: Changes in Types of Rural–Urban Food Remittances to Harare, 2008–2012

	2008 (% of recipient households)	2012 (% of recipient households)
Cereals	95	80
Vegetables	35	18
Roots or tubers	9	23
Fruit	5	24
Source: AFSUN		

CASE STUDY TWO
RECIPROCAL URBAN-RURAL REMITTING: NAMIBIA

Even in "normal times" urban migrant households rely to varying degrees on an informal, non-marketed food remittances to survive in precarious urban environments. One detailed study of 305 households in the poorer areas of Windhoek found that 85% of respondents (household heads) were migrants to Windhoek and that rural-urban migration was creating dynamic socio-economic relationships between the city and the rural north of the country.[66] A component of this "reciprocal social economy" linking urban and rural households (or nodes of the same household) in Namibia was urban-rural remitting of goods and especially cash. The practice of cash remitting has a long history in Namibia but is certainly not ubiquitous. In 2001, for example, 37% of urban households had remitted cash in the previous year, the same proportion as in 1991.[67] However, given Windhoek's dramatic growth during the 1990s, this means that the absolute number of rural households receiving cash remittances continued to increase. Half of those remitting cash did so at least once per quarter. Remittances were largely spent on school fees, healthcare and the purchase of foodstuffs in rural areas. In 2008, rates of cash remitting had increased to 52% of households and 90% of cash remittances went to the rural north of the country.[68]

Levels of urban food insecurity in Windhoek were lower than expected given pervasive poverty, high unemployment, a relatively small informal economy and scant evidence of urban agriculture.[69] Strong and resilient urban-rural social networks had ameliorated the food insecurity of poor urban households. The resources required to satisfy immediate food needs came predominantly from the rural areas direct to the urban household outside market channels. The most vulnerable households were those with weaker rural connections. Sixty-two percent of the households had received food remittances from rural relatives in the year prior to the survey and 58% received remittances 2 to 6 times per year. Produce received by the urban households included millet (received by 42% of households), wild foods (41%), and meat and fish (9%). The vast majority of households consumed the food themselves, with only 6% selling any of it. In Windhoek, therefore, urban food security for economically marginal households was dependent to a large degree on food remittances. However, the reciprocal flow of remittances from Windhoek was critical for rural livelihoods:

> *The flow of goods between the urban and rural areas is truly reciprocal. With about two-thirds of urban households both sending money to the rural areas and receiving food from rural households, the rural-urban symbiosis is well established. Unless there is rapid economic growth with jobs for unskilled and semi-skilled workers in Windhoek, the flow of food into the urban areas is likely to continue as urban households continue to diversify their sources of food and income.[70]*

Some have suggested that in reciprocal remitting the amount of money sent does not depend on the amount of food received.[71] In that sense, the system is not based on true reciprocity but on other variables such as available income and rural needs, in the case of cash remitting, and the absence of cash to buy food and the nature of the harvest, in the case of food remitting.

The practice of reciprocal remitting was confirmed in AFSUN's 2008 survey of 513 households in formal and informal settlements in Windhoek.[72] Again, there was a strong migration connection with 49% of households consisting exclusively of migrants, 40% comprising a mix of migrants and non-migrants (mainly children born in the city) and only 11% in which all members were non-migrants. A total of 41% of surveyed households had received food remittances from relatives in rural areas in the previous year. Of these, nearly 80% received cereals (primarily millet), 27% meat and poultry and 19% milk and milk products (Table 12). Rates of receipt of vegetables and fruit were much lower. The frequency of remitting varied with the type of food involved. For example, more than half of the households received cereals 3 to 6 times per year (Table 13). This suggests that remitting does not only occur after the harvest but also at other times, presumably from household stores. Products less tied to the agricultural calendar, such as meat and poultry and milk and milk products, still tend to be remitted more frequently. Fish and vegetables are remitted much less frequently.

Table 12: Types of Rural–Urban Food Remittance to Windhoek, 2008

	% of recipient households
Cereals	79
Meat and poultry	27
Milk and milk products	19
Legumes	13
Vegetables	12
Oils, fats, butter	4
Fruits	3
Eggs	1
Roots or tubers	0.5
Source: AFSUN	

Table 13: Frequency of Rural–Urban Food Remitting to Windhoek, 2008

	Cereals (% of recipient households)	Meat/poultry (% of recipient households)	Milk products (% of recipient households)	Fish (% of recipient households)	Vegetables (% of recipient households)
At least once per week	1	2	0	0	0
At least every two months	24	56	42	17	17
3–6 times per year	56	29	30	38	26
At least once per year	19	13	12	45	57
Source: AFSUN					

Households receiving food remittances from the rural areas emphasize that they are important for household survival. In the AFSUN survey, only a tiny minority (2.8%) indicated that the food received was unimportant to the household (Figure 6). The rest reported varying degrees of significance, with as many as 52% saying they were very important and 15% that they were critical to household survival. Interestingly, of the 11 Southern African cities surveyed by AFSUN, poor Windhoek residents spent the lowest proportion of their income on food. Indeed, in Windhoek's informal settlements, it appears, paradoxically, that in proportional terms "the poorer you are the less you actually spend on food."[73] This seems to confirm the self-assessment of the importance of food remitting to urban food security.

Figure 6: Self-Assessment of Importance of Food Remittances in Windhoek

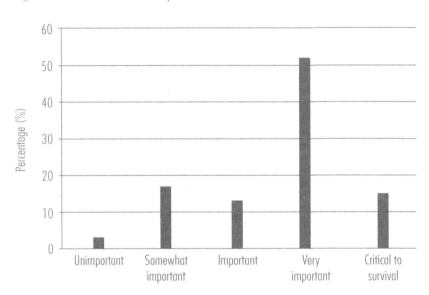

Source: AFSUN

Some broader hypotheses about rural-urban food remitting for testing in other contexts are suggested by the work on Windhoek. The first concerns the relationship between urban income and poverty and food remittances. In general, there is a strong relationship between household income and food security status in Windhoek.[74] But is there also a relationship between income and food remittances? A cross-tabulation of the amount of millet received by household income found that the poorest households received the greatest average amounts of millet.[75] At the same time, the relationship was relatively weak since households receiving millet were spread across income categories, prompting the overall conclusion that in poor areas of the city high income levels do not translate into lower transfers of food, at least among poorer households.[76] In the AFSUN survey, there was a slight decline in the importance of food remitting with increased income. For example, 35% of households receiving food remittances from rural relatives were in the lowest income tercile, 33% were in the middle tercile and 31% were in the upper tercile. A complete assessment of the frequency of food remitting across all income groups would require a city-wide survey, rather than one that focused on poor neighbourhoods only.

The second hypothesis is that food remittances improve food security and that we should therefore expect higher rates of remittance receipt among less food insecure households. But the 2008 AFSUN regional data set found that food transfers were particularly important for food-insecure households and that this relationship was statistically significant.[77] In total, only 16% of recipient households were food secure compared with 84% who were food insecure. Overall, the AFSUN data set showed that "the migration status of a household is not statistically correlated with an improvement in food security status."[78] Cross-tabulating household food security (as measured by the HFIAS) with food remittances in Windhoek gave exactly the same results as for the 11 city data set as a whole: 16% of recipient households were food secure and 84% were food insecure. This suggests that food remittances probably do make households less food insecure but that they are a response to acute insecurity and insufficient in quantity and regularity to guarantee a household's overall food security.

Third, is food remitting tied to the strength of the links that urban households maintain with rural areas? Over the generational long term, as the South African case makes clear, permanent urbanization and the loosening of rural linkages is likely to lead to the decline and eventual demise of food remitting. At the other end of the spectrum, as in Namibia, linkages remain very strong, not only in terms of material transfers but also through personal visits and interactions. Over 80% of households send someone to visit their relatives in the rural areas at least once a year, and many even more frequently. Reasons include special family events and also to participate in farming-related activities. There has been an argument that the length of time spent in Windhoek has no impact on the strength of ties to the rural areas.[79] This contrasts with the more personal but cynical view of one migrant that "in today's life you cannot rely on your own family elsewhere to support you because when you are working you are regarded as family but when you are not working then you are on your own."[80] To test this hypothesis more rigorously it would be necessary to collect data on a range of linkage types and then to correlate these with the frequency of food remittance receipts.

Fourth, there is considerable inter-household variation in levels of food security within the same geographical area of the city (Table 14). For example, food security levels are significantly higher in formal versus informal areas of Windhoek.[81] Within the informal areas, there are also significant variations by household type. The most food secure households are nuclear and male-centred (both male-headed). Both tend to be more food secure than extended family households, but the most food insecure are clearly female-headed households. More research is needed on how the characteristics of the household, such as size, location and demography, impact on food remitting from the countryside, and these characteristics need to be related to a similar range of characteristics of the rural household.

Table 14: Levels of Food Insecurity, Windhoek

	Formal areas	Informal settlements	Types of household in informal settlements			
			Female-centred households	Male-centred households	Nuclear households	Extended households
Food secure	29	8	4	10	9	8
Mildly food insecure	7	4	3	3	9	2
Moderately food insecure	14	13	7	15	12	18
Severely food insecure	50	76	85	72	71	71
Source: AFSUN						

Fifth, there is the issue of gender, food insecurity and food remittances and the particular vulnerability to poverty and food insecurity of female-centred households. In-depth interviews with female heads of household in Windhoek found a consistent pattern of exclusion, labour market discrimination and economic hardship among female-centred migrant households in the poorer areas of the city: "female-centred households are far more vulnerable than nuclear, male and extended households. Gender discrimination in the labour market means female heads of households are forced to adopt other livelihood strategies including informal selling of food as well as beer brewing, wood selling and sex work."[82] Extremely high levels of food insecurity translate into great anxiety and uncertainty about household food supply: asked how often over the previous month they had worried about whether the household would have enough food, 56% of female household heads said they were often or sometimes worried. Most households had adjusted their food intake in some way: 62% had sometimes or often eaten smaller meals because of a lack of resources; 55% had cut the number of meals due to a lack of food; 55% had sometimes or often had no food in the house; 47% had gone to sleep hungry due to lack of food; and 45% had gone a whole day and night without eating. But the proportion of households receiving food remittances was not significantly higher for female-centred households.[83] Another study in the rural north found no evidence of gender discrimination in the amounts of food remitted to Windhoek.[84]

Finally, do reciprocal remitting patterns change over time and, if so, why? At the household level, for example, is the volume and value of food and cash remitting dependent on the life cycle of the multi-spatial household? Does remitting tend to decline with length of urban residence? Do cash remittances increase and food remittances decrease if the urban household can secure a regular income through stable employment? At the regional level, are there longer-term trends in rural agriculture that are affecting rural production and therefore the amounts of food available to remit? And, if agriculture is in decline as it is in many other rural areas in Southern Africa, is this because of social, economic or environmental factors? Certainly, there was an apparent decline in food remittances between 2000 and 2008 (from 58% to 44% of recipient households). The reasons for this are not clear, though some migrants suggested that their links with the rural areas remain strong, but "out-migration and environmental changes (are) making rural agriculture less productive and causing a decline in the flow of food to Windhoek."[85]

CONCLUSIONS

The research literature and policy discussions on the impact of migrant remittances – at global, regional and national scales – focus almost exclusively on cash remitting. Connections between remittances and food tend to be confined to discussions of the impact of cash remittances on rural agricultural production and the widespread use of cash remittances by recipients to purchase food. The remitting of goods, and especially foodstuffs, across international boundaries and within countries has received little attention primarily, it seems, because these flows occur outside market channels. The result is that there is not much solid information on the volume, value and impacts of food remitting. This report reviews the available evidence for Africa, but it is clear that food remitting is a major research gap that demands much greater attention and a systematic, comparative programme of primary research.

The growing literature on urban-rural linkages has highlighted the complexity and dynamism of these connections in the context of rapid urbanization and greatly increased rural-urban migration in Africa. However, informal food remittances as a form of linkage have been neglected in favour of discussions on formal, market-based interactions and other types of flows. But the urban-rural linkages literature has important implications for understanding the practice of food remitting. First, linkages tend to be bidirectional in nature. Cash remittances tend to be unidirectional (from urban to rural), but food remittances are often bidirectional, with fresh produce flowing one way and processed foods the other. Alternatively, there is an element of reciprocity, with cash remittances flowing one way and food remittances the other. Second, the literature suggests that the urban-rural binary is arbitrary, outdated and unhelpful. Certainly it is hard to avoid these terms in describing remittances but it must be within the context of "a complex web of relations and connections incorporating rural and urban dimensions and all that is in between."[86] Food remitting cannot be treated in isolation from this complex web. Third, at the household level, the notion of the stretched or multi-nodal household is an extremely useful starting point for examining the drivers and impacts of food remitting at both urban and rural ends of the spectrum.

Several key findings emerge from the existing research literature on food remitting. First, there is considerable spatial variability in the volumes, frequency and types of foodstuffs that flow to the towns and cities for reasons that are not yet clear, given that many towns and cities have equally poor and food insecure populations. For example, it is clear why rural-urban food remitting is unimportant in South Africa where nearly 70% of the population is urbanized and the rural smallholder population is extremely impoverished. But why would there be such a large difference between Windhoek and Maputo, for example, when both have strong connections to the countryside? Second, the evidence suggests that rural-urban food flows tend to focus more on poor urban neighbourhoods and households than middle- and upper-income areas and are important to bolstering their food security.

On the other hand, there is some evidence that better-off rural households remit more than their less well-off counterparts. There have been no large-scale systematic studies that look simultaneously at the rural and the urban nodes of a household and chart the actual food pathways between them. Most of the existing research has been conducted either in the cities or in the countryside, not both. Third, we know a reasonable amount about the importance of food remitting to urban food security but little about what it means for rural food security in terms both of food sent and received. Finally, while it is important to focus on the rural-urban dimensions of food remitting, we should not ignore the fact that there are other significant dimensions of food remitting that are relatively unexplored, including rural-rural and urban-urban remitting.

The two case studies presented in this report are designed to highlight different facets of food remitting with potentially broader applicability. The first case study, of Harare in Zimbabwe, looks at food remittances under conditions of extreme economic and political duress. Zimbabwe's economic meltdown after 2000 is probably unprecedented but many African countries are no strangers to economic crisis, civil strife and, in some cases, state failure. The significance of food remitting to the urban poor in a state in crisis is amply demonstrated by the Harare case. In addition, the case study allows an assessment of the impact on food remitting with macro-economic and political stability. Clearly, without significant improvement in employment levels, incomes and the cost of food, the amelioration of a crisis, in itself, will have only a marginal impact on the significance of food remitting. The Windhoek case study provides an important example of cash remittances for food remittances reciprocity. At the same time, it raises a set of hypotheses about food remittances that need further elaboration and testing. These include the relationship between urban poverty and the level of food remitting; whether food remittances substantially reduce levels of urban food insecurity; if the volume and frequency of food remitting is related to the strength of the other links that urban residents maintain with the rural end; the reasons for inter-household variation in levels of food security and food receipts within the same geographical area of the city; the apparent greater vulnerability of female-centred households despite the lack of evidence for gender discrimination in food remitting; and whether reciprocal remitting patterns change over time with increased migration and urbanization.

The massive global attention paid to cash remittances over the past decade has provided an extremely solid evidence base for policymaking and advocacy at the international, regional and national level. Policy prescriptions for maximizing the flow and impacts of cash remittances on development are now legion and part of a growing policy consensus that remittances can be mainstreamed into development planning and the practices of the private sector, for the benefit of both senders and recipients, whether individuals, communities or whole countries. No equivalent knowledge base or policy dialogue exists with regard to food remittances. Much additional research on this important, yet much-neglected, aspect of urban-rural linkage and informal cross-order transaction is therefore urgently required. By drawing attention to the importance of food remittances for urban and rural food security and identifying the current knowledge gaps, this report creates a platform for the design of a new research agenda.

ENDNOTES

1 World Bank, "Migration and Remittances."

2 McKay and Deshingkar, "Internal Remittances and Poverty."

3 Adams, "Evaluating the Economic Impact of International Remittances"; Adams and Page, "Do International Migration and Remittances Reduce Poverty."

4 Adams, "Evaluating the Economic Impact of International Remittances"; Adams and Cuecuecha, "Impact of Remittances on Investment and Poverty"; Combes and Ebeke, "Remittances and Household Consumption Instability"; Fajnzylber and Humberto Lopez, *Remittances and Development*; Kapur, "Remittances: The New Development Mantra?"; Orozco and Ellis, "Impact of Remittances in Developing Countries"; Ratha et al, *Leveraging Migration for Africa*; Singh et al, "Determinants and Macroeconomic Impact of Remittances."

5 Abdih et al, "Remittances and Institutions"; Ahmed, "Remittances Deteriorate Governance"; Azam and Gubert, "Migrants' Remittances and the Household"; Rao and Hassan, "Panel Data Analysis of the Growth Effects of Remittances"; Rao and Hassan, "Direct and Indirect Growth Effects of Remittances."

6 Clemens et al, "Migration and Development Research."

7 Crush, "Linking Migration, Development and Urban Food Security."

8 Lacroix, "Migration, Rural Development, Poverty and Food Security"; Mendola, "Rural Out-Migration and Economic Development"; Zezza, "Assessing the Impact of Migration."

9 Karamba et al, "Migration and Food Consumption Patterns"; Lacroix, "Migration, Rural Development, Poverty and Food Security"; Nguyen and Winters, "Impact of Migration on Food Consumption Patterns."

10 Abadi et al, "Impact of Remittances on Household Food Security"; Crush and Pendleton, "Remitting for Survival"; Generoso, "How Do Rainfall Variability, Food Security and Remittances Interact"; Olowa et al, "Effects of Remittances on Poverty"; Regmi et al, "Impact of Remittance on Food Security"; Rosser, "Children's Consumption of Migration."

11 Babatunde and Qaim, "Impact of Off-Farm Income on Food Security"; Owusu et al, "Non-Farm Work and Food Security."

12 Karamba et al, "Migration and Food Consumption Patterns."

13 Adams, "Evaluating the Economic Impact of International Remittances"; Yang, "Migrant Remittances."

14 Todoroki et al, *The Canada-Caribbean Remittance Corridor.*

15 Crawford, "Sending Love in a Barrel."

16 Simmons et al, "Remittance Sending Practices of Haitians and Jamaicans."

17 Andersson Djurfeldt, "Multi-Local Livelihoods and Food Security" p. 540.

18 Berdegué et al, "The Rural Transformation".

19 Tacoli and Vorley, "Reframing the Debate."

20 Tacoli, "Rural-Urban Interactions."

21 Bah et al, "Changing Rural–Urban Linkages"; Berdegué and Proctor, "Inclusive Rural-Urban Linkages"; de Brauw et al, "Role of Rural-Urban Migration in Structural Transformation"; Proctor, "Rural Economic Diversification"; Steinberg, "Rural-Urban Linkages"; Tacoli, *Earthscan Reader in Rural-Urban Linkages*; Tacoli, "Poverty, Inequality and the Underestimation of Rural-Urban Linkages."

22 Tacoli, "Poverty, Inequality and the Underestimation of Rural-Urban Linkages"; see also Lerner and Eakin, "Rethinking the Rural–Urban Interface."

23 Potts, *Circular Migration.*

24 Andersson Djurfeldt, "Multi-Local Livelihoods and Food Security"; Francis, *Changing Livelihoods in Rural Africa.*

25 Tacoli, "Rural-Urban Interactions."

26 Andersson Djurfeldt, "Multi-Local Livelihoods and Food Security" p. 529.

27 Anich et al, *New Perspective on Human Mobility in the South*; Ratha et al, *Leveraging Migration for Africa.*

28 World Bank, *Migration and Remittances Factbook.*

29 Pendleton et al, *Migration, Remittances and Development.*

30 Plaza et al, *Migration and Remittances Household Surveys.*

31 Afrika and Ajumbo, "Informal Cross Border Trade in Africa"; FEWSNET, "Informal Cross Border Food Trade"; Golub, "Informal Cross-Broder Trade and Smuggling"; Lesser and Moisé-Leeman, "Informal Cross-Border Trade"; Peberdy et al, *Calibrating Informal Cross-Border Trade*; Sarris and Morrison, *Food Security in Africa.*

32 Akinboade, "Women, Poverty and Informal Trade Issues"; Mutopo, "Women Trading in Food"; Njikam and Tchouassi, "Women in Informal Cross-Border Trade."

33 Pendleton et al, *Migration, Remittances and Development.*

34 Crush et al, *Migration, Remittances and 'Development' in Lesotho*; Leduka et al, *State of Poverty and Food Insecurity in Maseru*; Turner, "Promoting Food Security in Lesotho."

35 Frayne and Pendleton, "The Development Role of Remittances in the Urbanization Process in Southern Africa."

36 Vearey et al, "HIV, Migration and Urban Food Security."

37 Frayne, "Migration and Urban Survival Strategies" p. 489.

38 Owuor, "Rural Livelihood Sources for Urban Households"; Owuor, "Migrants, Urban Poverty and the Changing Nature of Urban-Rural Linkages."

39 Frayne et al, *State of Urban Food Security in Southern Africa*.

40 Frayne, "Pathways of Food."

41 Ibid.

42 Andersson Djurfeldt and Wambugu, "In-Kind Transfers of Maize"; Andersson Djurfeldt, "Multi-Local Livelihoods and Food Security"; Andersson Djurfeldt, "Urbanization and Linkages to Smallholder Farming"; Djurfeldt et al, *African Smallholders*.

43 Andersson Djurfeldt, "Multi-Local Livelihoods and Food Security" p. 535

44 Ibid., p. 536.

45 Andersson Djurfeldt, "Multi-Local Livelihoods and Food Security."

46 Andersson Djurfeldt and Wambugu, "In-Kind Transfers of Maize" pp. 457-8.

47 Andersson, "Maize Remittances."

48 Ibid., p. 19.

49 Kuuire et al, "'Abandoning' Farms in Search of Food."

50 Ibid.

51 Andersson, "Reinterpreting the Rural–Urban Connection"; Andersson Djurfeldt, "Virtuous and Vicious Cycles in Rural-Urban Linkages"; Potts "Urban Unemployment and Migrants in Africa"; Potts, *Circular Migration*; Potts, "Internal Migration in Zimbabwe"; Potts and Mutambirwa, "Rural Urban Linkages in Contemporary Harare."

52 Chan and Primorac, *Zimbabwe in Crisis*; Chiumbu and Musemwa, *Crisis! What Crisis?*; Derman and Kaarhuis, *In the Shadow of a Conflict*.

53 Chaumba, "Social Capital and Employment Outcomes"; Chikanda and Crush, *Heading North*; Crush and Tevera, *Zimbabwe's Exodus*; Forrest et al, "Middle-Class Diaspora"; McGregor and Primorac, *Zimbabwe's New Diaspora*; Pasura, *African Transnational Diasporas*.

54 Potts, "Urbanization and Migrancy in an Imploding Economy"; Potts, "Internal Migration in Zimbabwe."

55 Tawodzera, "Vulnerability and Resilience in Crisis"; Tawodzera, "Vulnerability in Crisis"; Tawodzera, "Urban Household Survival and Resilience"; Tawodzera, "Rural-Urban Transfers and Household Food

Security"; Tawodzera, "Household Food Insecurity and Survival in Harare"; Tawodzera et al, *State of Food Insecurity in Harare.*

56 Tawodzera et al, *State of Food Insecurity in Harare.*

57 Tawodzera, "Vulnerability and Resilience in Crisis."

58 Tawodzera, "Rural-Urban Transfers and Household Food Security" p. 5.

59 Ibid., p. 6.

60 Tawodzera, "Vulnerability and Resilience in Crisis."

61 Tawodzera, "Rural-Urban Transfers and Household Food Security."

62 Ibid.

63 Newfarmer and Pierola, *Trade in Zimbabwe.*

64 Tawodzera et al, State of Food Insecurity in Harare.

65 Tawodzera, "Household Food Insecurity and Survival in Harare."

66 Frayne, "Survival of the Poorest: Food Security and Migration in Namibia."

67 Frayne, "Migration and Urban Survival Strategies in Windhoek."

68 Pendleton et al, "Migrant Windhoek."

69 Frayne, "Rural Productivity and Urban Survival"; Frayne, "Survival of the Poorest: Migration and Food Security in Namibia"; Frayne, "Migration and the Changing Social Economy of Windhoek."

70 Frayne, "Survival of the Poorest: Food Security and Migration in Namibia" p. 278.

71 Guettou and Djurfeldt, "Gender and Access to Food" p. 36.

72 Pendleton et al, "Migrant Windhoek."

73 Nickanor, "Food Deserts and Household Food Insecurity" pp. 108-9.

74 Frayne, "Pathways of Food" p. 306.

75 Frayne, "Migration and the Changing Social Economy of Windhoek."

76 Frayne, "Rural Productivity and Urban Survival" p. 66.

77 Frayne, "Pathways of Food" p. 300.

78 Ibid.

79 Pomuti and Tvedten, *Namibia: Urbanization in the 1990s.*

80 Nickanor, "Food Deserts and Household Food Insecurity" p. 173.

81 Nickanor, "Food Deserts and Household Food Insecurity."

82 Nickanor, "Food Deserts and Household Food Insecurity" p. 189.

83 Nickanor, "Food Deserts and Household Food Insecurity."

84 Guettou and Djurfeldt, "Gender and Access to Food" p. 45.

85 Nickanor, "Food Deserts and Household Food Insecurity" p. 169.

86 Tacoli, "Poverty, Inequality and Underestimation of Rural-Urban Linkages."

REFERENCES

1.   Abadi, N., Techane, A., Tesfay, G., Maxwell, D. and Vaitla, B. (2013). "The Impact of Remittances on Household Food Security: A Micro Perspective from Tigray, Ethiopia" Department of Natural Resource Economics and Management, Mekelle University, Ethiopia.

2.   Abdih, Y., Chami, R., Dagher, J. and Montiel, P. (2012). "Remittances and Institutions: Are Remittances a Curse?" *World Development* 40: 657-666.

3.   Adams, R. (2011). "Evaluating the Economic Impact of International Remittances On Developing Countries Using Household Surveys: A Literature Review" *Journal of Development Studies* 47: 809-828.

4.   Adams, R. and Cuecuecha, A. (2013). "The Impact of Remittances on Investment and Poverty in Ghana" *World Development* 50: 24-40.

5.   Adams, R. and Page, J. (2005). "Do International Migration and Remittances Reduce Poverty in Developing Countries?" *World Development* 33: 1645-1669.

6.   Afrika, J-G. and Ajumbo, G. (2012). "Informal Cross Border Trade in Africa: Implications and Policy Recommendations" Africa Economic Brief 3, African Development Bank.

7.   Ahmed, F. (2013). "Remittances Deteriorate Governance" *Review of Economics and Statistics* 95: 1166-1182.

8.   Akinboade, O. (2005). "A Review of Women, Poverty and Informal Trade Issues in East and Southern Africa" *International Social Science Journal* 57: 255-275.

9.   Andersson, A. (2011). "Maize Remittances, Smallholder Livelihoods and Maize Consumption in Malawi" *Journal of Modern African Studies* 49: 1-25.

10. Andersson, J. (2001). " Reinterpreting the Rural–Urban Connection: Migration Practices and Socio-Cultural Dispositions of Buhera Workers in Harare" *Africa* 71: 82-112.

11. Andersson Djurfeldt, A. (2012). "Virtuous and Vicious Cycles in Rural-Urban Linkages: Cases from Zimbabwe" *Africa Review* 4: 136-156.

12. Andersson Djurfeldt, A. (2015a). "Multi-Local Livelihoods and Food Security in Rural Africa" *Journal of International Development* 27: 528-545.

13. Andersson Djurfeldt, A. (2015b). "Urbanization and Linkages to Smallholder Farming in Sub-Saharan Africa: Implications for Food Security" *Global Food Security* 4:1-7.

14. Andersson Djurfeldt, A. and Wambugu, S. (2011). "In-Kind Transfers of Maize, Commercialization and Household Consumption in Kenya" *Journal of Eastern African Studies* 5: 447-464.

15. Anich, R., Crush, J., Melde, S. and Oucho, J. (eds.) (2014). *A New Perspective on Human Mobility in the South* (London and Geneva: Springer and IOM).

16. Azam, J-P. and Gubert, F. (2006). "Migrants' Remittances and the Household in Africa: A Review of Evidence" *Journal of African Economies* 15: 426-462.

17. Babatunde, R. and Qaim, M. (2010). "Impact of Off-Farm Income on Food Security and Nutrition in Nigeria" *Food Policy* 35: 303-311.

18. Bah, M., Cissè, S., Divamett, B., Diallo, G., Lerise, F., Okali, D., Okpara, E., Olawoye, J. and Tacoli, C. (2003). "Changing Rural–Urban Linkages in Mali, Nigeria and Tanzania" *Environment and Urbanization* 15: 13-24.

19. Berdegué, J. and Proctor F. (2014). "Inclusive Rural-Urban Linkages" Working Paper No. 123, Territorial Cohesion for Development Program. Rimisp, Santiago, Chile.

20. Berdegué. J., Rosada, T. and Bebbington, A. (2014). "The Rural Transformation" In B. Currie-Adler, R. Kanbur, D. Malone and R. Medhora (eds.) *International Development: Ideas, Experience, and Prospects* (Oxford: Oxford University Press), pp. 463-78.

21. Chan, S., and Primorac, R. (2007). *Zimbabwe in Crisis: The International Response and the Space of Silence.* New York: Routledge.

22. Chaumba, J. 2015. "Social Capital and Employment Outcomes of Zimbabwean Immigrants in the United States" *Journal of International Migration and Integration* DOI:10.1007/s12134-015-0419-z.

23. Chikanda, A. and Crush, J. (2012). *Heading North: The Zimbabwean Diaspora in Canada.* SAMP Migration Policy Series No. 62, Cape Town.

24. Chikanda, A. and Crush, J. (2014). "Diasporas of the South" In R. Anich, J. Crush, S. Melde and J. Oucho (eds.), *A New Perspective on Human Mobility in the South* (London and Genva: Springer and IOM), pp. 65-88.

25. Chiumbu, S. and Musemwa, M. (eds.) (2012). *Crisis! What Crisis? The Multiple Dimensions of the Zimbabwean Crisis.* Cape Town: HSRC.

26. Clemens, M., Özden, Ç. and Rapoport, H. (2014). "Migration and Development Research is Moving Far Beyond Remittances" *World Development* 64: 121-124.

27. Combes, J-L. and Ebeke, C. (2011). "Remittances and Household Consumption Instability in Developing Countries" *World Development* 39: 1076-1089.

28. Crawford, C. (2003) "Sending Love in a Barrel: The Making of Transnational Caribbean Families in Canada" *Canadian Woman Studies* 22: 104-109.

29. Crush, J. (2013). "Linking Migration, Development and Urban Food Security" *International Migration* 51: 61-75.

30. Crush, J. and Pendleton, W. (2009). "Remitting for Survival: Rethinking the Development Potential of Remittances" *Global Development Studies* 5(3-4): 1-28.

31. Crush, J. and Tevera, D. (eds.) (2010). *Zimbabwe's Exodus: Crisis, Migration, Survival*. Cape Town and Ottawa: SAMP and IDRC.

32. Crush, J., Dodson, B., Gay, J., Green, T. and Leduka, C. (2010). *Migration, Remittances and 'Development' in Lesotho*. SAMP Migration Policy Series No. 52, Cape Town.

33. de Brauw, A., Mueller, V. and Lee, H. (2014). "The Role of Rural-Urban Migration in the Structural Transformation of Sub-Saharan Africa" *World Development* 63: 33-42.

34. Derman, B., and Kaarhuis, R. (eds.) (2013). *In the Shadow of a Conflict: Crisis in Zimbabwe and Its Effects in Mozambique, South Africa and Zambia*. Harare: Weaver.

35. Dodson, B., Chiweza, A. and Riley, L. (2012). *Gender and Food Insecurity in Southern African Cities*. AFSUN Urban Food Security Series No. 10, Cape Town.

36. Djurfeldt, G., Aryeetey, E. and Isinika, A. (eds.) (2011). *African Smallholders: Food Crops, Markets and Policy*. Cambridge, MA: CAB International.

37. Fajnzylber, P. and Humberto Lopez, J. (eds.) (2008). *Remittances and Development: Lessons from Latin America* (Washington DC: World Bank).

38. FEWSNET (2012). "Informal Cross Border Food Trade in Southern Africa" Pretoria, South Africa.

39. Forrest, J., Johnston, R. and Poulsen, M. (2013). "Middle-Class Diaspora: Recent Immigration to Australia from South Africa and Zimbabwe" *South African Geographical Journal* 95: 50-69.

40. Francis, E. (2000). *Making a Living: Changing Livelihoods in Rural Africa* (London: Routledge).

41. Frayne, B. (2001). "Survival of the Poorest: Food Security and Migration in Namibia" PhD Thesis, Queen's University, Kingston.

42. Frayne, B. (2004). "Migration and Urban Survival Strategies in Windhoek, Namibia" Geoforum 35: 489-505.

43. Frayne, B. (2005a). "Rural Productivity and Urban Survival in Namibia: Eating Away from Home" *Journal of Contemporary African Studies* 23: 51-76.

44. Frayne, B. (2005b). "Survival of the Poorest: Migration and Food Security in Namibia" In L. Mougeot (ed.), *Agropolis: The Social, Political and Environmental Dimensions of Urban Agriculture* (Ottawa: IDRC), pp. 32-50.

45. Frayne, B. (2007). "Migration and the Changing Social Economy of Windhoek, Namibia" *Development Southern Africa* 26: 91-108.

46. Frayne, B. (2010). "Pathways of Food: Mobility and Food Transfers in Southern African Cities" *International Development Planning Review* 32: 291-310.

47. Frayne, B. and Pendleton, W. (2009). "The Development Role of Remittances in the Urbanization Process in Southern Africa" *Global Development Studies* 5: 85-132.

48. Frayne, B., Pendleton, W., Crush, J. et al (2010). *The State of Urban Food Security in Southern Africa*. AFSUN Urban Food Security Series No. 2, Cape Town.

49. Generoso, R. (2015). "How Do Rainfall Variability, Food Security and Remittances Interact? The Case of Rural Mali" *Ecological Economics* 114: 188-198.

50. Golub, S. (2015). "Informal Cross-Broder Trade and Smuggling in Africa" In O. Morrissey, R. López and K. Sharma (eds.), *Handbook on Trade and Development* (Cheltenham: Edward Elgar), pp. 179-209.

51. Guettou, N. and Djurfeldt, A. (2014). "Gender and Access to Food: A Case Study on Gender Differences in Access to Food through Rural to Urban Food Transfers, and Its Impact on Food Security in Moses //Garoëb, Windhoek, Namibia" MSc Thesis, Lund University, Sweden.

52. Kapur, D. (2004). "Remittances: The New Development Mantra?" G-24 Discussion Paper Series No. 29, UNCTAD, New York.

53. Karamba, W., Quiñones, E. and Winters, P. (2011). "Migration and Food Consumption Patterns in Ghana" *Food Policy* 36: 41-53.

54. Kuuire, V., Mkandawire, P., Arku, G. and Luginaah, I. (2013). "'Abandoning' Farms in Search of Food: Food Remittance and Household Food Security in Ghana" *African Geographical Review* 32: 125-139.

55. Lacroix, T. (2011). "Migration, Rural Development, Poverty and Food Security: A Comparative Perspective" International Migration Institute, Oxford University, Oxford.

56. Leduka, R., Crush, J., Frayne, B., McCordic, C., Matobo, T., Makoa, T., Mphale, M., Phaila, M. and Letsie, M. (2015). *The State of Poverty and Food Insecurity in Maseru, Lesotho*. AFSUN Urban Food Security Series No. 21, Cape Town.

57. Lerner, A. and Eakin, H. (2010) "An Obsolete Dichotomy? Rethinking the Rural–Urban Interface in Terms of Food security and Production in the Global South" *Geographical Journal* 177: 311-320.

58. Lesser, C. and Moisé-Leeman, E. (2009). "Informal Cross-Border Trade and Trade Facilitation Reform in Sub-Saharan Africa" OECD Trade Policy Papers No. 86, OECD Publishing, Paris.

59. McGregor, J. and Primorac, R. (eds.) (2010). *Zimbabwe's New Diaspora: Displacement and the Cultural Politics of Survival*. New York and Oxford: Berghahn Books.

60. McKay, A. and Deshingkar, P. (2014) "Internal Remittances and Poverty: Further Evidence from Africa and Asia" Migrating Out of Poverty Working Paper No. 12, Sussex University, Brighton.

61. Mendola, M. (2012). "Rural Out-Migration and Economic Development at Origin: A Review of the Evidence" *Journal of International Development* 24: 102-122.

62. Mutopo, P. (2010). "Women Trading in Food Across the Zimbabwe-South Africa Border: Experiences and Strategies" *Gender and Development* 18: 465-477.

63. Newfarmer, R. and Pierola, M. (2015). *Trade in Zimbabwe: Changing Incentives to Enhance Competitiveness*. Washington DC: World Bank.

64. Nickanor, N. (2013). "Food Deserts and Household Food Insecurity in the Informal Settlements of Windhoek, Namibia" PhD Thesis, University of Cape Town, South Africa.

65. Nguyen, M. and Winters, P. (2011). "The Impact of Migration on Food Consumption Patterns: The Case of Vietnam" *Food Policy* 36: 71-87.

66. Njikam, O. and Tchouassi, G. (2011). "Women in Informal Cross-Border Trade: Empirical Evidence from Cameroon" *International Journal of Economics and Finance* 3: 202-213.

67. Olowa, W., Awoyemi, T., Shittu, A. and Olowa, A. (2013). "Effects of Remittances on Poverty among Rural Households in Nigeria" *African Journal of Agricultural Research* 8: 872-883.

68. Orozco, M. and Ellis, C., (2014). "Impact of Remittances in Developing Countries" In R. Anich, J. Crush, S. Melde and J. Oucho (eds.) *A New Perspective on Human Mobility in the South* (New York: Springer and Geneva: IOM), pp. 89-118.

69. Owuor, S. (2003). "Rural Livelihood Sources for Urban Households: A Study of Nakuru Town" Working Paper No. 51, African Studies Centre, Leiden.

70. Owuor, S. (2010). "Migrants, Urban Poverty and the Changing Nature of Urban-Rural Linkages in Kenya" In J. Crush and B. Frayne (eds.), *Surviving on the Move: Migration, Poverty and Development in Southern Africa* (Midrand: DBSA), pp. 117-31.

71. Owusu, V., Abdulai, A. and Abdul-Rahman, S. (2011). "Non-Farm Work and Food Security Among Farm Households in Northern Ghana" *Food Policy* 3: 108-118.

72. Pasura, D. (2014). *African Transnational Diasporas: Fractured Communities and Plural Identities of Zimbabweans in Britain*. Basingstoke: Palgrave Macmillan.

73. Peberdy, S., Crush, J., Tevera, D., Campbell, E., Raimundo, I., Tsoka, M., Zindela, N., Tawodzera, G., Nickanor, N., Mulenga, C., Green, T., and Msibi, N. (2014). *Calibrating Informal Cross-Border Trade in Southern Africa*, SAMP Migration Policy Series No. 69, Cape Town.

74. Pendleton, W., Crush, J., Campbell, E., Green, T., Simelane, H., Tevera, D. and de Vletter, F. (2006). *Migration, Remittances and Development in Southern Africa*. SAMP Policy Series No, 44, Cape Town.

75. Pendleton, W., Crush, J. and Nickanor, N. (2014). "Migrant Windhoek: Rural–Urban Migration and Food Security in Namibia" *Urban Forum* 25: 191-205.

76. Plaza, S., Navarrete M. and Ratha, D. (2011). *Migration and Remittances Household Surveys: Methodological Issues and New Findings from Sub-Saharan Africa* (Washington, DC: World Bank).

77. Pomuti, A. and Tvedten, I. (1998). *Namibia: Urbanization in the 1990s* (Windhoek: NEPRU).

78. Potts, D. (2000). "Urban Unemployment and Migrants in Africa: Evidence from Harare, 1985-1994" *Development and Change* 31: 879-910.

79. Potts, D. (2006). "'All My Hopes and Dreams are Shattered': Urbanization and Migrancy in an Imploding Economy: Zimbabwe in the 21st Century" *Geoforum* 37: 536-51.

80. Potts, D. (2010a). *Circular Migration in Zimbabwe and Contemporary Sub-Saharan Africa* (London: James Currey).

81. Potts, D. (2010b). "Internal Migration in Zimbabwe: The Impact of Livelihood Destruction in Rural and Urban Areas" In J. Crush and D. Tevera (eds.), *Zimbabwe's Exodus: Crisis, Migration, Survival* (Ottawa: ISRC), pp. 79-111.

82. Potts, D. and Mutambirwa, C. (1990). Rural Urban Linkages in Contemporary Harare: Why Migrants Need Their Land" *Journal of Southern African Studies* 16: 677-98.

83. Proctor, F. (2014) "Rural Economic Diversification in Sub-Saharan Africa" IIED Working Paper, London.

84. Rao, B. and Hassan, G. (2011). "A Panel Data Analysis of the Growth Effects of Remittances" *Economic Modelling* 28: 701-709.

85. Rao, B. and Hassan, G. (2012). "Are the Direct and Indirect Growth Effects of Remittances Significant?" *The World Economy* 35: 351-372.

86. Ratha, D., Mohapatra, S., Ozden, C., Plaza, S., Shaw, W. and Shimeles, W. (2011). *Leveraging Migration for Africa: Remittances, Skills, and Investments* (Washington DC: World Bank).

87. Regmi, M., Paudel, K. and Mishra, A. (2015). "Impact of Remittance on Food Security in Bangladesh" Department of Agricultural Economics and Agribusiness, Louisiana State University, Baton Rouge, LA.

88. Rosser, E. (2011). "Children's Consumption of Migration: Remittances and Food Security" *Border-Lines* 5.

89. Sarris, A. and Morrison, J. (2010). *Food Security in Africa: Market and Trade Policy for Staple Foods in Eastern and Southern Africa*. Rome and Cheltenham: FAO and Edward Elgar.

90. Simmons, A., Plaza, D. and Piché, V. (2005). "The Remittance Sending Practices of Haitians and Jamaicans in Canada" Centre for Research on Latin America and the Caribbean, York University, Toronto.

91. Singh, R., Haacker, M., Lee, K. and Le Goff, M. (2010). "Determinants and Macroeconomic Impact of Remittances in Sub-Saharan Africa" *Journal of African Economies* 20: 312-340.

92. Steinberg, F. (2011). "Rural-Urban Linkages: An Urban Perspective" Working Paper No. 128, Territorial Cohesion for Development Program, RIMISP, Santiago.

93. Tacoli, C. (1998). "Rural-Urban Interactions: A Guide to the Literature" *Environment and Urbanization* 10: 147-166.

94. Tacoli, C. (ed.) (2006). *The Earthscan Reader in Rural-Urban Linkages* (London: Earthscan).

95. Tacoli, C. (2007). "Poverty, Inequality and the Underestimation of Rural-Urban Linkages" *Development* 50: 90-95.

96. Tacoli, C. and Vorley, B. (2015). "Reframing the Debate on Urbanisation, Rural Transformation and Food Security" IIED Briefing, London.

97. Tawodzera, G. (2010). "Vulnerability and Resilience in Crisis: Urban Household Food Insecurity in Harare, Zimbabwe" PhD Thesis, University of Cape Town, South Africa.

98. Tawodzera, G. (2011). "Vulnerability in Crisis: Urban Household Food Insecurity in Epworth, Harare, Zimbabwe" *Food Security* 3: 503-520.

99. Tawodzera, G. (2012). "Urban Household Survival and Resilience to Food Insecurity in Crisis Conditions: The Case of Epworth in Harare, Zimbabwe" *Journal of Hunger and Environmental Nutrition* 7: 293-320.

100. Tawodzera, G. (2013). "Rural-Urban Transfers and Household Food Security in Harare's Crisis Context" *Journal of Food & Nutritional Disorders* 2: 1-10.

101. Tawodzera, G. (2014). "Household Food Insecurity and Survival in Harare: 2008 and Beyond" *Urban Forum* 25: 207-216.

102. Tawodzera, G., Zanamwe, L. and Crush, J. (2012). *The State of Food Insecurity in Harare, Zimbabwe*. AFSUN Urban Food Security Series No. 13, Cape Town.

103. Todoroki, E., Vaccai, M. and Noor, W. (2009). "The Canada-Caribbean Remittance Corridor" Working Paper No. 163, World Bank, Washington DC.

104. Turner, S. (2009). "Promoting Food Security in Lesotho: Issues and Options" Priority Support Programme, Maseru.

105. Vearey, J., Núñez, L. and Palmary, I. (2009). "HIV, Migration and Urban Food Security: Exploring the Linkages" Forced Migration Studies Programme, Wits University, Johannesburg.

106. World Bank (2015). *Migration and Remittances Factbook: 2016*, World Bank, Washington DC.

107. Yang, D. (2011). "Migrant Remittances" *Journal of Economic Perspectives* 25: 129–152.

108. Zezza, A., Carletto, C., Davis, B. and Winters, P. (2011). "Assessing the Impact of Migration on Food and Nutrition Security" *Food Policy* 36: 1-6.

MIGRATION POLICY SERIES

1   *Covert Operations: Clandestine Migration, Temporary Work and Immigration Policy in South Africa* (1997) ISBN 1-874864-51-9

2   *Riding the Tiger: Lesotho Miners and Permanent Residence in South Africa* (1997) ISBN 1-874864-52-7

3   *International Migration, Immigrant Entrepreneurs and South Africa's Small Enterprise Economy* (1997) ISBN 1-874864-62-4

4   *Silenced by Nation Building: African Immigrants and Language Policy in the New South Africa* (1998) ISBN 1-874864-64-0

5   *Left Out in the Cold? Housing and Immigration in the New South Africa* (1998) ISBN 1-874864-68-3

6   *Trading Places: Cross-Border Traders and the South African Informal Sector* (1998) ISBN 1-874864-71-3

7   *Challenging Xenophobia: Myth and Realities about Cross-Border Migration in Southern Africa* (1998) ISBN 1-874864-70-5

8   *Sons of Mozambique: Mozambican Miners and Post-Apartheid South Africa* (1998) ISBN 1-874864-78-0

9   *Women on the Move: Gender and Cross-Border Migration to South Africa* (1998) ISBN 1-874864-82-9.

10 *Namibians on South Africa: Attitudes Towards Cross-Border Migration and Immigration Policy* (1998) ISBN 1-874864-84-5.

11 *Building Skills: Cross-Border Migrants and the South African Construction Industry* (1999) ISBN 1-874864-84-5

12 *Immigration & Education: International Students at South African Universities and Technikons* (1999) ISBN 1-874864-89-6

13 *The Lives and Times of African Immigrants in Post-Apartheid South Africa* (1999) ISBN 1-874864-91-8

14 *Still Waiting for the Barbarians: South African Attitudes to Immigrants and Immigration* (1999) ISBN 1-874864-91-8

15 *Undermining Labour: Migrancy and Sub-Contracting in the South African Gold Mining Industry* (1999) ISBN 1-874864-91-8

16 *Borderline Farming: Foreign Migrants in South African Commercial Agriculture* (2000) ISBN 1-874864-97-7

17 *Writing Xenophobia: Immigration and the Press in Post-Apartheid South Africa* (2000) ISBN 1-919798-01-3

18 *Losing Our Minds: Skills Migration and the South African Brain Drain* (2000) ISBN 1-919798-03-x

19 *Botswana:˙Migration Perspectives and Prospects* (2000) ISBN 1-919798-04-8

20 *The Brain Gain: Skilled Migrants and Immigration Policy in Post-Apartheid South Africa* (2000) ISBN 1-919798-14-5

21 *Cross-Border Raiding and Community Conflict in the Lesotho-South African Border Zone* (2001) ISBN 1-919798-16-1

22 *Immigration, Xenophobia and Human Rights in South Africa* (2001) ISBN 1-919798-30-7

23 *Gender and the Brain Drain from South Africa* (2001) ISBN 1-919798-35-8

24 *Spaces of Vulnerability: Migration and HIV/AIDS in South Africa* (2002) ISBN 1-919798-38-2

25 *Zimbabweans Who Move: Perspectives on International Migration in Zimbabwe* (2002) ISBN 1-919798-40-4

26 *The Border Within: The Future of the Lesotho-South African International Boundary* (2002) ISBN 1-919798-41-2

27 *Mobile Namibia: Migration Trends and Attitudes* (2002) ISBN 1-919798-44-7

28 *Changing Attitudes to Immigration and Refugee Policy in Botswana* (2003) ISBN 1-919798-47-1

29 *The New Brain Drain from Zimbabwe* (2003) ISBN 1-919798-48-X

30 *Regionalizing Xenophobia? Citizen Attitudes to Immigration and Refugee Policy in Southern Africa* (2004) ISBN 1-919798-53-6

31 *Migration, Sexuality and HIV/AIDS in Rural South Africa* (2004) ISBN 1-919798-63-3

32 *Swaziland Moves: Perceptions and Patterns of Modern Migration* (2004) ISBN 1-919798-67-6

33 *HIV/AIDS and Children's Migration in Southern Africa* (2004) ISBN 1-919798-70-6

34 *Medical Leave: The Exodus of Health Professionals from Zimbabwe* (2005) ISBN 1-919798-74-9

35 *Degrees of Uncertainty: Students and the Brain Drain in Southern Africa* (2005) ISBN 1-919798-84-6

36 *Restless Minds: South African Students and the Brain Drain* (2005) ISBN 1-919798-82-X

37 *Understanding Press Coverage of Cross-Border Migration in Southern Africa since 2000* (2005) ISBN 1-919798-91-9

38 *Northern Gateway: Cross-Border Migration Between Namibia and Angola* (2005) ISBN 1-919798-92-7

39 *Early Departures: The Emigration Potential of Zimbabwean Students* (2005) ISBN 1-919798-99-4

40 *Migration and Domestic Workers: Worlds of Work, Health and Mobility in Johannesburg* (2005) ISBN 1-920118-02-0

41 *The Quality of Migration Services Delivery in South Africa* (2005) ISBN 1-920118-03-9

42 *States of Vulnerability: The Future Brain Drain of Talent to South Africa* (2006) ISBN 1-920118-07-1

43 *Migration and Development in Mozambique: Poverty, Inequality and Survival* (2006) ISBN 1-920118-10-1

44 *Migration, Remittances and Development in Southern Africa* (2006) ISBN 1-920118-15-2

45 *Medical Recruiting: The Case of South African Health Care Professionals* (2007) ISBN 1-920118-47-0

46 *Voices From the Margins: Migrant Women's Experiences in Southern Africa* (2007) ISBN 1-920118-50-0

47 *The Haemorrhage of Health Professionals From South Africa: Medical Opinions* (2007) ISBN 978-1-920118-63-1

48 *The Quality of Immigration and Citizenship Services in Namibia* (2008) ISBN 978-1-920118-67-9

49 *Gender, Migration and Remittances in Southern Africa* (2008) ISBN 978-1-920118-70-9

50 *The Perfect Storm: The Realities of Xenophobia in Contemporary South Africa* (2008) ISBN 978-1-920118-71-6

51 *Migrant Remittances and Household Survival in Zimbabwe* (2009) ISBN 978-1-920118-92-1

52 *Migration, Remittances and 'Development' in Lesotho* (2010) ISBN 978-1-920409-26-5

53 *Migration-Induced HIV and AIDS in Rural Mozambique and Swaziland* (2011) ISBN 978-1-920409-49-4

54 *Medical Xenophobia: Zimbabwean Access to Health Services in South Africa* (2011) ISBN 978-1-920409-63-0

55 *The Engagement of the Zimbabwean Medical Diaspora* (2011) ISBN 978-1-920409-64-7

56 *Right to the Classroom: Educational Barriers for Zimbabweans in South Africa* (2011) ISBN 978-1-920409-68-5

57 *Patients Without Borders: Medical Tourism and Medical Migration in Southern Africa* (2012) ISBN 978-1-920409-74-6

58 *The Disengagement of the South African Medical Diaspora* (2012) ISBN 978-1-920596-00-2

59 *The Third Wave: Mixed Migration from Zimbabwe to South Africa* (2012) ISBN 978-1-920596-01-9

60 *Linking Migration, Food Security and Development* (2012) ISBN 978-1-920596-02-6

61 *Unfriendly Neighbours: Contemporary Migration from Zimbabwe to Botswana* (2012) ISBN 978-1-920596-16-3

62 *Heading North: The Zimbabwean Diaspora in Canada* (2012) ISBN 978-1-920596-03-3

63 *Dystopia and Disengagement: Diaspora Attitudes Towards South Africa* (2012) ISBN 978-1-920596-04-0

64 *Soft Targets: Xenophobia, Public Violence and Changing Attitudes to Migrants in South Africa after May 2008* (2013) ISBN 978-1-920596-05-7

65 *Brain Drain and Regain: Migration Behaviour of South African Medical Professionals* (2014) ISBN 978-1-920596-07-1

66 *Xenophobic Violence in South Africa: Denialism, Minimalism, Realism* (2014) ISBN 978-1-920596-08-8

67 *Migrant Entrepreneurship Collective Violence and Xenophobia in South Africa* (2014) ISBN 978-1-920596-09-5

68 *Informal Migrant Entrepreneurship and Inclusive Growth in South Africa, Zimbabwe and Mozambique* (2015) ISBN 978-1-920596-10-1

69 *Calibrating Informal Cross-Border Trade in Southern Africa* (2015) ISBN 978-1-920596-13-2

70 *International Migrants and Refugees in Cape Town's Informal Economy* (2016) ISBN 978-1-920596-15-6

71 *International Migrants in Johannesburg's Informal Economy* (2016) ISBN 978-1-920596-18-7

Printed in the United States
By Bookmasters